D0501483

WITHDRAWN

The Green Berets

by Tom Streissguth

Capstone Press

MINNEAPOLIS

Printed in the United States of America.

Capstone Press • 2440 Fernbrook Lane • Minneapolis, MN 55447

Editorial Director   John Coughlan
Managing Editor   Tom Streissguth
Production Editor   James Stapleton
Book Design   Tim Halldin

Library of Congress Cataloging-in-Publication Data

Streissguth, Thomas, 1958-
    The Green Berets / by Tom Streissguth
        p. cm. -- (Serving your country)
    Includes bibliographical references (p. 44) and index.
    Summary: A short history of the U.S. Army's Special
Forces and an explanation of the training required to
become a Green Beret.
    ISBN 1-56065-283-7
    1. United States. Army. Special Forces--Juvenile
literature. [1. United States. Army. Special Forces.]
I. Title. II. Series.
    UA34.S64S77   1996
    356'.167'0973--dc20   95-439
                                                CIP
                                                AC

Table of Contents

Chapter 1

In Action

It's late at night. A light rain is falling, hiding the sound of your footsteps. You're happy to have that sound, because you're spending the night deep behind enemy lines–by yourself.

As a member of the Special Forces, you're prepared. You had some of the toughest training in the United States military. You can survive for days, even weeks if necessary, with little food or sleep. You know how to treat a

Green Beret training prepares soldiers for action behind enemy lines.

Mapping and radio communication are important skills to have for Special Forces missions.

gunshot wound, communicate with radios, telegraphs, or mirrors, and speak the language of the country where you're fighting. You also know weapons, explosives, and hand-to-hand combat.

You also know how to raise a friendly **guerrilla** force and turn it against your enemy. After all, this was the reason for the founding of the Special Forces. The first mission for the members of this elite team–who are also known as the Green Berets–was to train guerrilla forces to fight the enemies of the United States.

During World War II (1939-1945), Special Operations Groups–the first Special Forces–**sabotaged** enemy roads, bridges, railroads, and fortifications. They recruited remote tribes in the jungles of Burma to fight the Japanese. And they prepared for invasions by the regular Army and Marine Corps against German armies in Europe. Later, during the Vietnam War of the 1960s, Green Berets trained Vietnamese farmers and villagers to take on the **Viet Cong**, a skillful guerrilla force.

It wasn't a job for the regular Army. Most regular soldiers don't have the skill or endurance needed for combat and survival behind enemy lines. The Special Forces take only volunteers, and many of those who do volunteer never make it through the training course. Those who qualify wear their Special Forces **insignia** with great pride.

Here is the story of the Green Berets–how they began, what they have accomplished, and how they train their members today.

Chapter 2

How the Green Berets Began

The first special operations forces saw action during World War II (1939-1945). They were part of the Office of Strategic Services, or OSS. The OSS was responsible for **espionage** and sabotage. To carry out its mission, the group formed a special operations group.

A sergeant wears the traditional black beret as well as the insignia of the 7th Special Forces Group.

The slogan of the Special Forces, De Oppresso Liber, means "To Free from Tyranny" in Latin.

There were 30 enlisted men and three officers in each group. They trained for combat behind enemy lines. They learned how to handle explosives and how to survive in the wilderness. They also became experts in hand-to-hand fighting and radio communications.

In Europe, the OSS put several teams to work in France and Italy. The teams destroyed German railroads, power plants, and military units. In Burma, a country in Asia, special operations led Burmese fighters against the forces of Japan.

After the war, the Special Forces groups became 12-man teams, also known as A-teams. They trained for guerrilla fighting in the wild Chattahochee National Forest. There, some members of the Special Forces began wearing black berets. Later, all Special Forces would wear green berets. This is the origin of the name Green Berets. But this is just a nickname–the official name of these groups is still the Special Forces.

Vietnam

In the early 1960s, the United States began sending military forces to the Asian nation of Vietnam. There, Communist guerrillas were trying to overthrow the government of South Vietnam, an ally of the U.S. By the mid-1960s, there was fighting throughout South Vietnam. The Special Forces would play an important part in this conflict.

The key mission of the Special Forces was to train South Vietnamese guerrillas to fight against the **Communists**, who were also known as the Viet Cong. Special Forces teams would recruit these guerrillas in the countryside, where they would set up training camps. The Green Berets also worked near the borders of South Vietnam to stop weapons and guerrillas from crossing into the country.

Later in the war, Special Forces camps were set up far from the main areas of fighting. These camps were meant to survive on their own, even if the Viet Cong surrounded them.

During a scouting mission, a Special Forces sergeant studies a field map to plot his course through the forest.

They were protected by heavy guns and could be supplied from the air. The men in the camps went on dangerous missions to fight the Viet Cong and disrupt the enemy's supply.

The Special Forces also organized the **Mobile Strike Force**. About 600 men made up one of these units. The Mobile Strike Force

During the Vietnam War, Special Forces troops were prepared for jungle warfare.

could carry out raids and ambushes against the enemy. In case of a Viet Cong attack, the unit could be quickly sent to the scene for a counterattack.

Mobile guerrilla forces were also organized to carry out attacks on the Viet Cong. These were smaller units that could survive for up to two months in the jungles of Vietnam. The men were trained to sabotage enemy camps and **ammunition dumps**. They received their food, ammunition, and other supplies from the air.

By 1970, the U.S. began shutting down the Special Forces camps. The military began turning the war back over to the army of South Vietnam. Vietnamese guerrillas trained by the Green Berets joined the regular South Vietnamese army. Most U.S. Special Forces soldiers went back to the United States. In all, 544 U.S. Special Forces soldiers lost their lives during the war.

In 1974, the United States pulled the rest of its military out of the country. Soon afterward, the Viet Cong defeated South Vietnam.

A group of Kuwaiti soldiers receives Special Forces training during the Persian Gulf War of 1991.

Chapter 3

The Modern Special Forces

Special Forces teams had more missions after the end of the Vietnam War. Disaster Assistance and Relief teams flew all over the world. Their assignment was to help people at the scene of a natural disaster. Doctors and medical assistants cared for the injured, while other members of the teams help set up camps and kitchens.

Special Forces training prepares soldiers for survival under dangerous, difficult conditions.

A combat-control team radios coordinates and positions to headquarters.

The Green Berets also worked as advisors to governments allied with the United States. They trained foreign soldiers and officers in guerrilla warfare. The United States sent Special Forces teams to the South American

nations of Chile, Colombia, Venezuela, and the
Dominican Republic.

These teams were carrying on the fight
against Communism, which the U.S. still saw
as a threat to its allies. The Green Berets
helped these nations to fight against
Communist guerrillas in the cities and
countryside. A Bolivian unit trained by the
Special Forces captured and killed Che
Guevara, one of the world's most famous
revolutionary guerrilla leaders.

The Delta Force

When citizens of the United States are in
trouble abroad, sometimes the Special Forces
are called on to help. One of the most famous
rescue missions took place in the Middle
Eastern nation of Iran.

In 1979, a violent revolution against the
shah (ruler) of Iran took place. The shah fled
the country as the revolution brought down his
government. The shah had been a close ally of
the United States. For this reason, the leaders

of Iran's revolution were enemies of the United States government.

Later that year, a crowd of people stormed into the United States embassy in Teheran, the capital of Iran. They took over the building and captured 44 Americans. For months, these **hostages** were held prisoner on the embassy grounds. The U.S. government was unable to free them.

To rescue the hostages, the U.S. military drew up a secret plan. The code name for the plan was Operation Eagle Claw. The plan called for using a Special Forces unit called the **Delta Force**. This team had first seen action during the Vietnam War. It was trained to kidnap enemy leaders, carry out nighttime raids, and rescue U.S. prisoners held by the Viet Cong.

For Operation Eagle Claw, the Delta Force prepared to land in a desert far from the Iranian capital. The team would then drive into

A Special Forces group sets out on patrol during training at Fort Bragg, North Carolina.

Teheran under cover, raid the embassy, and bring out the 44 hostages. To train and prepare for the raid, the Delta Force spent several weeks in Arizona, where conditions were similar to the deserts of Iran.

The Raid

On the night of April 24, 1980, U.S. helicopters and supply planes flew into Iran. Although the Delta Force was ready for action, the helicopters weren't prepared for a sudden sandstorm that came up during the night. The storm forced some of the helicopters to turn back.

Several planes and helicopters did make it to Desert One, the code name for the landing site. But with only six choppers left, the leaders of the operation decided there were no longer enough men to carry out Operation Eagle Claw. They decided to abort, or stop the mission.

While taking off from Desert One, one of the helicopters suddenly crashed into a supply plane on the ground. There was a loud

Special Forces teams are trained and equipped for house-to-house fighting.

explosion of fuel and ammunition. Eight soldiers died in the blast. Although they had performed bravely, the members of the mission were unable to rescue the hostages.

Low-Intensity Conflicts

After the breakup of the Soviet Union in the early 1990s, the U.S. government no longer saw Communism as a threat to its allies.

Instead of another world war, the military began to prepare for a different kind of war, which its leaders called low-intensity conflicts.

These were wars between smaller states, or civil conflict between a government and rebels who might be trying to overthrow it. With their training in guerrilla warfare, and their readiness to fight in many different areas of the world, the Green Berets were well prepared to take part in these low-intensity conflicts.

One such violent area was Haiti. A very poor country in the Caribbean Sea, Haiti has suffered civil war and political violence for many years. In 1994, the United States supported a new Haitian government, which would replace a strict military **dictatorship**.

To help the new government, the U.S. sent in several Special Forces teams. The Green Berets helped Haitians build new roads, schools, and houses. In this way, the United States hoped to make the new government more popular among Haitians.

The results of this peaceful mission are still uncertain. Although the Special Forces can

The Eisenhower, a U.S. aircraft carrier, sails for Haiti with a group of Special Forces teams in 1995.

train others to help themselves, the military is not prepared to take part in Haiti's political conflict. If Haitians can peacefully resolve their differences, the Special Forces mission there will be a success.

Chapter 4

Becoming a Green Beret

The Special Forces are still part of the United States Army, but Special Forces training is different from the regular Army course. Special Forces teams only take volunteers. Only men between the ages of 17 and 35 are accepted for the training course. You also have to be a high school graduate and in good physical condition.

A trainee prepares for scouting and surveillance missions.

All Special Forces training takes place at Fort Bragg, a military base in North Carolina. The first part of the course includes physical training. This means running, hiking, marching, pushups, pullups, situps, and other exercises. The first stage also includes

Oxygen masks are used in high-altitude jump training.

airborne training. Trainees learn how to jump from a height, how to control a parachute in the air, and how to land after a jump without injury.

They take their first jumps while on a **static line**. Instead of pulling the chutes open by hand, they attach the chutes to a line inside the plane. As they leap, the line opens the chute automatically.

The Qualification Course

This is the next step in becoming a member of the Green Berets. At the Qualification Course, trainees learn how to survive and fight in the wilderness. They climb steep hillsides and **rappel**–let themselves down the hill again with a rope. They learn how to use a compass and how to find their way over rough and wooded land. Instructors also show them how to fight hand-to-hand and how to **ambush** the enemy. There are more parachute jumps and practice in leading guerrilla forces in enemy territory.

The Qualification Course holds a very tough challenge. Trainees must go into the woods by themselves, with only a knife, a book of matches, rain gear, and a rabbit or a chicken. With this equipment and food, they must survive for three days on their own.

Proper care of weapons and equipment is an important part of all military training.

Finally the trainees make a 12-mile march while carrying 45-pound backpacks. If they finish the march within three hours, they've passed the course.

Specialties

After the Qualification Course, a trainee is officially qualified to become a member of the Special Forces. But he must choose a specialty—an area of military training that interests him. There are five different specialties.

In Communications, trainees learn how to handle all kinds of radio gear. They learn Morse code, which is used to send messages. They also repair radios, telephones, and other electronic equipment.

In Demolitions and Engineering, trainees learn how to use explosives, mines, and **booby traps** to destroy bridges, buildings, fortifications, roads, and many other military

Many Special Forces members train for work in communications.

targets. They also learn how to build and repair these targets.

Medical specialists learn how to treat injuries, especially combat injuries. They learn how to operate on patients, how to pull a tooth, and how to give medicines. This kind of training takes longer than any other specialty.

The Weapons specialist studies many different kinds of guns, including machine guns, pistols, revolvers, shotguns, and rifles. He practices on a shooting range to sharpen his **marksmanship.** He also learns how to repair and care for weapons.

In Operations and Intelligence, Special Forces teaches code-breaking, espionage (spying), training of guerrilla troops, photography, secret communications, and other skills that are important in carrying out a military campaign.

Chapter 5

The Special Forces Today

In 1987, the Special Operations Command was formed. This organization trains and commands all the special forces units of the United States military. The entire organization includes about 50,000 officers and soldiers, from Green Berets to Army Rangers to Navy SEALs.

Members of the 5th Special Forces Group run an obstacle course in the Middle East.

**Special Forces units
accept women in non-
combat roles**.

The Special Forces are organized into groups, each of which is responsible for a certain area of the world. Members of the group learn the language, geography, history, and politics of the area. This prepares them for the special problems they may find if they are sent to their region.

Although some people questioned the need for the Special Forces, there is no doubt that the United States will continue to support this organization. If the nation needs a highly skilled fighting force anywhere in the world, the Green Berets will be ready.

Ski troops can handle winter conditions and mountain terrain.

Glossary

airborne–military forces that are sent into battle by parachute

ambush–to stage a surprise attack on enemy forces

ammunition dump–a storage area for arms and explosives

booby trap–an explosive device designed to surprise and injure or kill an enemy soldier

Communist–a member or follower of Communism, which favors government control of the economy and single-party rule

Delta Force–a special military team trained to fight terrorism and rescue hostages

dictatorship–rule by a single person who allows no opposition

espionage–to carry out surveillance (spying) missions against another country

guerrilla–one who fights in a small force or alone, often behind enemy lines

hostage–a person taken prisoner by someone else, often for money

insignia–a design used by a military unit to identify its members

marksmanship–the ability to accurately fire a weapon

Mobile Strike Force–a force set up to carry out raids and ambushes during the Vietnam War

rappel–to go down a cliff or steep hillside using a rope

sabotage–to destroy enemy property or equipment

shah–a ruler of Iran before the revolution of 1979

static-line jump–to leap from a plane with the parachute attached to a rope, which opens the chute automatically

Viet Cong–Communist guerrilla forces fighting against the government of South Vietnam

To Learn More

Miller, David. *Modern Elite Forces.* New York: Smithmark Publishers, 1992.

Moran, Tom. *The U.S. Army.* Minneapolis: Lerner Publications, 1990.

Paradis, Adrian A. *Opportunities in Military Careers.* Lincolnwood, IL: VGM Career Horizons, 1989.

The Visual Dictionary of Special Military Forces. New York: Dorling Kindersley, Inc. 1993.

Walner, Max. *An Illustrated Guide to Modern Elite Forces.* New York: Arco, 1984.

Some Useful Addresses

U.S. Army Infantry Training Center
Fort Benning, GA   31905

United States Special Forces
Fort Bragg, NC   28307

Index